WELLNESS MATTERS
YOUR JOURNEY WITH MENTAL ILLNESS
& METABOLIC SYNDROME

Erica Alexandra Falk-Huzar
PsyD, EdS, MBA, HS-BCP

Foreword by Kyira Wackett, MS, LPC

WELLNESS MATTERS®
Your Journey with Mental Illness & Metabolic Syndrome

This handbook was created with the support of my wife, Brenda, my daughter, Merceydeis, my mother, Pamela, my sister, Kristina and my friend, Patty. A further acknowledgment goes out to my Scholarly Chair, Dr. Stein who helped me prepare for a life of psychological wellness.

TABLE OF CONTENTS

FOREWORD

When I first met Erica, I was still trying to find my voice. I was unsure of who I was and who I wanted to be in this world. I worked myself into the ground and was constantly inundated with "shoulds" and "supposed tos". Pressure to power through, produce more, and work beyond limits and boundaries is something that many of us have internalized throughout our lives and make the idea of self-care seem like a joke — a luxury far beyond my reach.

Erica has always been upfront about her own recovery and what life has looked like for her. We bonded over our ability to hyperextend ourselves and push beyond limits, motivated by our passion and drive to make the world a better, more inclusive space. We bonded over the self-loathing and shame that we can carry with us when we battle mental health and feel like our brain and bodies are fighting us or holding us back.

But in this, Erica also invited another possible self into the mix. The version of herself trying to find balance. The version working to see herself as worthy of taking care of herself and to see her own health and well-being as important not just so she can produce more and have a greater impact but because she was a part of the world we were working to change and deserved to find peace and joy within it.

We met while she was serving on the board for a non-profit mental health agency that I worked at and this discussion was something she brought into space a lot — how can we balance making meaningful change and doing hard work with taking care of ourselves? And how do we create a sense of community and connection so that people can see, feel and trust that they matter? How do we give people the tools to create their best life, building a team that can support them in their efforts rather than collude with the belief we are incapable or less than?

As Erica and I have continued on our own personal and professional paths, I have continued to be motivated by her drive and empowered by her willingness to find that balance. She is a testament to letting go of that sense of urgency and letting things happen in their own time. She has helped me see that it is about creating goals and pursuits that make you feel whole and that the timeline does not matter — what matters is making sure you can take care of yourself as well as the people you want to support in your life.

The only way to create a life we can thrive in is to take care of the body that we are in while we are alive. And, while many of us were dealt cards that make that process trickier to figure out — mental health issues, trauma, physical health issues including metabolic syndrome — we are both allowed and capable of figuring out what that means for us. If I, truly, want to be a change in the world, I have to model what it looks like to practice self-love and self-compassion. I have to help others see that they are worthy of taking up space and being seen by allowing myself to be seen as well. And we have to have the courage to be vulnerable enough to say we cannot do it all. The cost is too high. Only then can we see that we were never meant to but instead are a part of a community who, when we take care of ourselves and take care of each other, can create not only meaningful but deep and everlasting change in this world.

Thank you Erica for being a model of how to do this — how to show up for yourself and to be honest when you struggle or get pulled back into the pressure to do rather than be — and for being a light source for so many of us so that we can pull from your strength and guidance to do hard things.

With love and kindness as you, too, join the force working to future and love ourselves and to create a life we can thrive in.

Kyira Wackett, MS, LPC
Mental Health Therapist & Founder of Adversity Rising, LLC

PREFACE

During my time as a mental health professional and also as someone who lives with mental illness and metabolic syndrome, I found that resources regarding self-care are limited. This work is a product of my applied doctoral project after studying for years in psychology.

Creating and preparing this resource is not only beneficial for YOU, it is also beneficial for ME. While it can be used for mental health self-care in general, it is specifically geared toward individuals struggling with the two conditions or even at risk for the conditions.

Remember to share your questions, thoughts, and findings with your primary provider and/or your behavioral health practitioner for optimal results.

Enjoy and be well.

WHAT IS WELLNESS MATTERS?

How does the information in this handbook apply to you? Are you living with a mental illness and do you have symptoms of a physical condition such as obesity, high blood pressure, diabetes, or high cholesterol? Perhaps a doctor has told you that you have or are at risk for having metabolic syndrome? This is an educational wellness handbook that will help you learn and understand how your mental health affects your physical health and vice versa.

It is filled with facts, information, journaling prompts *and so much more.* You are free to choose to use any part of this handbook or the whole thing.

Living with a mental illness is complicated as it is. And now you have to worry about other health factors? Well, Wellness Matters is here to help you navigate these concerns and assist you in learning how to put these words into action. Having a mental illness puts you at risk for metabolic syndrome. Big words aside, what's important is taking care of yourself! By understanding how you can better care for yourself, you'll live happier and healthier.

On a scale from 0-10, with 0 being not at all likely and 10 being extremely likely, how would you rate the following?

How important is your health to you?

| 0 | 1 | 2 | 3 | 4 | 5 | 6 | 7 | 8 | 9 | 10 |

How ready are you to make a change in your life?

| 0 | 1 | 2 | 3 | 4 | 5 | 6 | 7 | 8 | 9 | 10 |

How confident are you that you can make a change?

| 0 | 1 | 2 | 3 | 4 | 5 | 6 | 7 | 8 | 9 | 10 |

What is Metabolic Syndrome?

Metabolic syndrome is a severe physical condition that reduces the quality of life of individuals and increases the chances of various diseases. It consists of a group of conditions that occur together, which increases the risk of heart disease, stroke, and diabetes. Conditions include increased blood pressure, high blood sugar, excess body fat around the waist, and abnormal cholesterol or triglyceride levels. The term is used to describe an unhealthy condition associated with various metabolism issues including hypertension, hyperglycemia, and obesity.

There is a strong correlation between metabolic syndrome and mental illness and there are so many factors that go into this. Part of the reason is the lack of self-care. We are more apt to focus only on our mental health and, I get it, it's difficult enough to deal with emotions. Other reasons include psychotropic medications and lifestyle factors.

What? What does all of this mean for you? Let's break it down. Individuals with mental illness are at greater risk for serious conditions. This can include:

- Heart disease
- Diabetes
- Obesity
- High cholesterol
- High blood pressure

Footnotes: Kelly et al., 2014; Bermudes, 2006; Cunningham et al, 2018; Kaur, 2014; Rojo et al., 2015; Gardner-Sood et al., 2015; Gill et al., 2016.

Why should this be important to me?
Taking care of yourself, and not just emotionally, can increase your lifespan and quality of life. Who wants to be at risk for these things? Let's see how we can help.

You may have heard of Wellness Wheels. While there are so many versions, I find that all have great purpose. For purposes of this handbook, we're going to focus on a personal Wellness Wheel for self-care that I find most "fitting" for individuals living with a mental health condition or just struggling with life in general. This wellness wheel has the following components: Healthy Eating, Exercise, Smoking Cessation, Stress-Reduction, and Integrative Therapy. Often, I've found that individuals (especially those dealing with mental health conditions) find it overwhelming to focus on so many aspects even if not all at once.

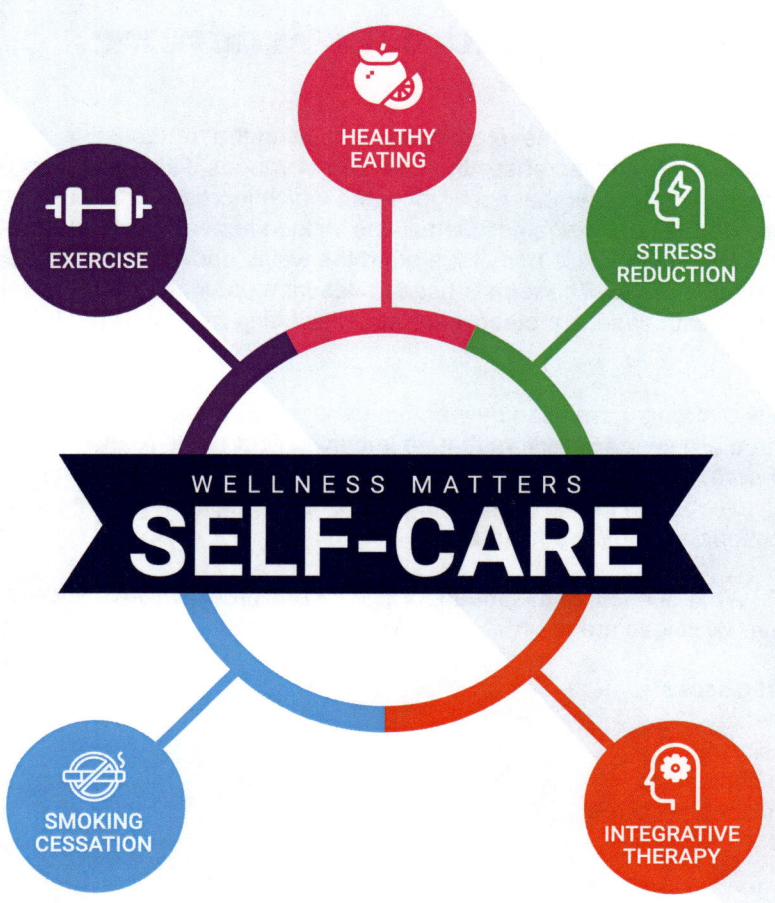

What are your reasons for wanting to be healthier?

_____
_____
_____

How can you measure success?

_____
_____
_____

What are your motivators?

_____
_____
_____

HEALTHY EATING

Healthy eating is one of the most important factors in treating and preventing metabolic syndrome because eating habits play a central role in its development. I bet you'd agree that it's no surprise individuals who live with mental illness often consume fast food and have eating habits that contribute to obesity and other problems. What can we do about this?

Food doesn't just nourish our bodies; it also affects our minds! A lack of any of the important nutrients can increase chances of metabolic syndrome and even affect the way our psychotropic medications are broken down. Did you know that not eating nutritionally can cause changes in brain functioning?? Seriously? Yes! Think about that and how much better individuals can feel if they're eating well or, at least, better. What you eat affects your daily life, mood, and energy levels. By following simple guidelines, you can ensure that you're taking care of your body AND your emotions, which all lead to better living with mental illness.

It's also no surprise that eating well can also lead to weight loss, which… you guessed it… helps prevent metabolic syndrome. To ensure you're eating the right number of calories for YOU, chat with your provider. They can help you determine how many calories you need a day to lose or maintain weight and to ensure you're healthy.

If you eat too little or too much, you can experience tiredness, irritability, sadness,
and more. Therefore, it's important to reduce sodium (see note below) and saturated fat intake and increase the consumption of vegetables, legumes, fruit, and other foods low on the glycemic index (GI). Fruits and vegetables contain a relatively small number of calories; however, they provide a feeling of "fullness" quicker than fast food. Furthermore, one of the main advantages of fruits and vegetables is that they are nutrient-dense foods containing many vitamins.

> **Are you prescribed Lithium?** Since lithium is a natural occurring mineral similar to salt, ensuring that you have a healthy daily salt intake is important. For example, if your provider told you that you are at a therapeutic level, but then you go and eat a whole bag of potato chips, your lithium level can decrease. We don't want that to happen! Be sure to consult with your provider regarding your diet when you are taking lithium.

Choosing the Right Foods *(Enlarged menu located at the back of the book for easy access.)*

GRAINS Make half your grains whole	VEGETABLES Vary your veggies	FRUITS Focus on fruits	MILK Get your calcium-rich foods	MEAT & BEANS Go lean with protein
Eat at least 3 oz. of whole-grain cereals, breads, crackers, rice, or pasta every day	Eat more dark-green veggies like broccoli, spinach, and other dark leafy greens	Eat a variety of fruit	Go low-fat or fat-free when you choose milk, yogurt, and other milk products	Choose low-fat or lean meats and poultry
1 oz. is about 1 slice of bread, about 1 cup of breakfast cereal, or ½ cup of cooked rice, cereal, or pasta	Eat more orange vegetables like carrots and sweetpotatoes Eat more dry beans and peas like pinto beans, kidney beans, and lentils	Choose fresh, frozen, canned, or dried fruit Go easy on fruit juices	If you don't or can't consume milk, choose lactose-free products or other calcium sources such as fortified foods and beverages	Bake it, broil it, or grill it Vary your protein routine — choose more fish, beans, peas, nuts, and seeds

For a 2,000-calorie diet, you need the amounts below from each food group. To find the amounts that are right for you, go to MyPyramid.gov.

Eat 6 oz. every day	Eat 2½ cups every day	Eat 2 cups every day	Get 3 cups every day; for kids aged 2 to 8, it's 2	Eat 5½ oz. every day

Find your balance between food and physical activity
- Be sure to stay within your daily calorie needs.
- Be physically active for at least 30 minutes most days of the week.
- About 60 minutes a day of physical activity may be needed to prevent weight gain.
- For sustaining weight loss, at least 60 to 90 minutes a day of physical activity may be required.
- Children and teenagers should be physically active for 60 minutes every day, or most days.

Know the limits on fats, sugars, and salt (sodium)
- Make most of your fat sources from fish, nuts, and vegetable oils.
- Limit solid fats like butter, margarine, shortening, and lard, as well as foods that contain these.
- Check the Nutrition Facts label to keep saturated fats, trans fats, and sodium low.
- Choose food and beverages low in added sugars. Added sugars contribute calories with few, if any, nutrients.

MyPyramid.gov
STEPS TO A HEALTHIER YOU

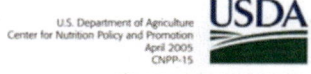

U.S. Department of Agriculture
Center for Nutrition Policy and Promotion
April 2005
CNPP-15

What about going out to eat? Should you not do that anymore? Of course, you can! There's nothing wrong with going out to eat… you should just be more aware of what you're ordering. And, don't forget that restaurants are pretty willing to accommodate your requests. Get baked fish instead of fried. Get steamed green beans, instead of fried. Get fat free milk, instead of whole milk. Be careful with buffets! While they're cheaper, challenge yourself to take one large plate of everything you want and then don't go for seconds. Remember: It takes about 20 minutes for your brain to say "Hey! I'm full" so take your time while eating!

Eating Out Plan

What do I usually eat when I go out?

_____

_____

_____

What can I do to change it up to be healthier?

_____

_____

_____

WHEN I GO TO:	
FOODS TO EAT	**FOODS NOT TO EAT**

WHEN I GO TO:	
FOODS TO EAT	**FOODS NOT TO EAT**

WHEN I GO TO:	
FOODS TO EAT	**FOODS NOT TO EAT**

Your short-term eating goals:

_____

_____

_____

Your long-term eating goals:

_____

_____

_____

Who will be your support person?

_____

_____

How will you reward yourself?

_____

_____

_____

These are some "yummy" and healthy foods I like now:

_____

_____

_____

These are some healthy foods I'd like to try:

_____

_____

_____

This is how I can include them in my diet:

_____

_____

_____

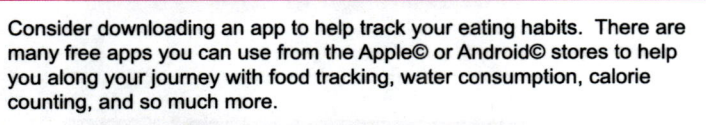

Consider downloading an app to help track your eating habits. There are many free apps you can use from the Apple© or Android© stores to help you along your journey with food tracking, water consumption, calorie counting, and so much more.

NOTES ALONG YOUR JOURNEY:

EXERCISE

Not only is exercise good for your physical health, but it is also good for your mental and emotional health.

Exercise can lower the risk of metabolic syndrome! What?! Seriously? Yes, it decreases your risk for high blood pressure, high cholesterol, weight gain, heart disease, and diabetes. While this all sounds great, how easy is it to exercise?

Is it difficult for you to get up and moving? While this may be one of your barriers, start small. Do some light warm-ups until you and your body are ready to move on.

Are you thinking it's too expensive? Nah, you don't need a gym membership. Move at home. Walk up and down the stairs instead of taking the elevator. Jog in place while watching your favorite movie. Once you've got this down, follow these steps to get you going:

WARM-UP	ADJUST TO A "KEEP UP" PACE (ABOUT 5-10 MINUTES)
STRENGTH TRAINING	A VARIETY OF WAYS (BURNS CALORIES AND INCREASES MUSCLE MASS)
AEROBIC EXERCISE	EXERCISE TO GET YOUR HEART GOING (REDUCES DEPRESSION AND ANXIETY)
FLEXIBILITY EXERCISES	STRETCHING IS AWESOME AND CAN BE FUN LIKE YOGA OR PILATES
COOL-DOWN	TAKE SOME TIME TO SLOWLY COOL DOWN (NEED SOME RECOUPING TIME)

Let's stop the judgement. Let's problem-solve. Write down a negative thought and then turn it into a positive thought.

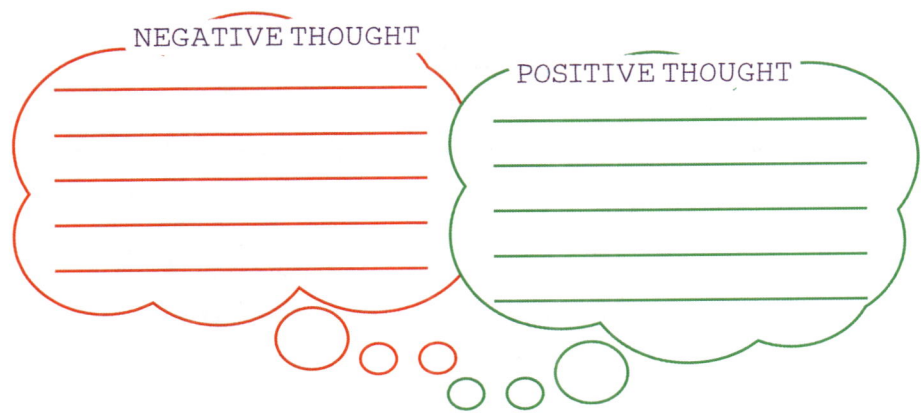

NEGATIVE THOUGHT

POSITIVE THOUGHT

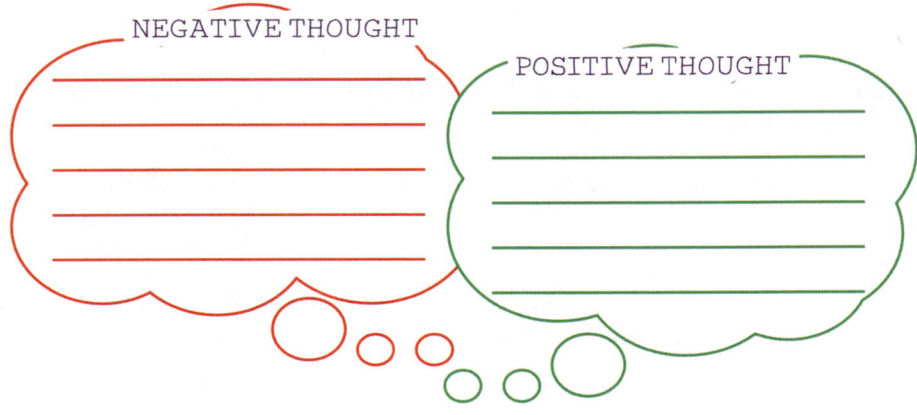

NEGATIVE THOUGHT

POSITIVE THOUGHT

Your short-term exercising goals:

_____
_____
_____
_____

Your long-term exercising goals:

_____
_____
_____
_____

These are some exercises I'd like to try:

_____
_____
_____
_____

This is what I'm going to do to reward myself:

_____
_____
_____

NOTES ALONG YOUR JOURNEY:

SMOKING CESSATION

Individuals with mental illness have a very high rate of smoking. Even though individuals living with mental illness are twice as likely to smoke, they also have a high-quit rate. This is great news for you! Why should you quit smoking? While the answer is obvious, we know that this feat is difficult for you! Think of these things:

- Within 20 minutes of quitting, your heart rate drops.
- After 12 hours, carbon monoxide levels drop to normal.
- After two weeks (to three months) your lung function improves and your risk for a heart attack begins to drop.
- After one (to nine) months, your coughing and shortness of breath decreases.
- After one year, the increased risk of coronary heart disease is that of HALF of a tobacco user.
- After five to fifteen years, your risk of stroke is reduced as if you were a nonsmoker.

What's all the hype about you may ask?? Smoking helps me with my anxiety! Smoking helps calm my hallucinations! While these things may feel true, the reality is that you'll be proud of completing a VERY difficult task! It's awesome for your self-esteem, which is what brings us to the "root" of this book!

On a scale from 0-10, with 0 being not al all likely and 10 being extremely likely, how would you rate the following?

How ready are you to quit?

0	1	2	3	4	5	6	7	8	9	10

How important is it for you to quit?

0	1	2	3	4	5	6	7	8	9	10

How confident are you that you can quit?

0	1	2	3	4	5	6	7	8	9	10

The reality is, you do not have "worse" symptoms after you quit and, evidence shows that, you may require lower doses of psychotropic medications because SMOKING increases the breakdown of your medication, which often means that you need higher doses of medications. How cool is that? Less meds = less side effects = increased health and happiness!

Deciding to quit and taking action:

Seeing the progress you are making toward your goals will encourage you to continue with your plan and keep you pushing forward reaching for a healthier lifestyle.

Drawbacks of smoking:

_____

_____

_____

_____

Your short-term goals:

_____

_____

_____

Your long-term goals:

_____

_____

_____

How do you plan to fight urges?

_____

_____

_____

Who will be your support person?

_____

_____

_____

_____

How will you reward yourself?

_____

_____

_____

_____

What are you going to do with all that money saved???

_____

_____

_____

_____

Do you need help?

_____

_____

_____

_____

There are many nicotine replacement options available.

TYPE	WHAT IS IT?	TRY IT?
TRANSDERMAL PATCH	THE NICOTINE PATCH IS A SKIN PATCH COATED WITH NICOTINE. IT IS AVAILABLE OVER-THE-COUNTER, AND SOME INSURANCES DO COVER IT.	O
GUM	THIS IS AN ORAL NICOTINE MEDICATION USED AS A TEMPORARY AID TO HELP YOU STOP SMOKING. YOU CHEW IT LIKE GUM AND THEN, FOR FULL EFFECT, SIT IT BETWEEN THE GUM AND CHEEK.	O
LOZENGES	THIS IS AN ORAL NICOTINE MEDICATION USED AS A TEMPORARY AID TO HELP YOU STOP SMOKING. THE LOZENGES SIT BETWEEN THE GUM AND CHEEK.	O
INHALER	THIS IS A NICOTINE MEDICATION USED BY INHALING NICOTINE INTO THE LUNGS. THIS WILL HELP CONTROL YOUR CRAVING AND MAY EVEN HELP WITH THE "HABIT" OF THE ACT.	O
NASAL SPRAY	THIS IS A NICOTINE NASAL SPRAY IF YOU WANT A NICOTINE REPLACEMENT OTHER THAN PATCHES, GUM, OR LOZENGE. THIS IS A PRESCRIPTION MEDICATION.	O

There are other non-nicotine replacement options, but we'll leave those questions and answers to your provider.

Let's do it! What's your quit date? _____/_____/_____

Consider downloading an app to help you with quitting. There are many free apps you can use from the Apple© or Android© stores for motivators, tracking your money savings, providing tips along the way, and more.

NOTES ALONG YOUR JOURNEY:

STRESS REDUCTION

Stress is typical for individuals with mental illness. Stress negatively affects various aspects of an individual's life and reduces help-seeking behavior and self-care. However, it is relatively simple for you to resist stress. It may sound difficult, but don't let it fool you!!

Identify five stressors or problems going on in your life right now and rank each one with "1" being the greatest stressor:

_____   _____

_____   _____

_____   _____

_____   _____

_____   _____

What are your triggers and how can we manage them?
1. Identify the trigger
2. Change the environment or your reaction
3. Create a solution (but make it reasonable and doable)

TRIGGER: _____

CHANGES: _____

SOLUTION: _____

TRIGGER: _____

CHANGES: _____

SOLUTION: _____

TRIGGER: _____

CHANGES: _____

SOLUTION: _____

One of the easiest ways to help you develop stress resistance is mindfulness-based interventions and mindfulness meditation. The concept of mindfulness has become quite popular in recent years and mindfulness-based interventions are very effective for stress reduction.

- What do I do to practice core mindfulness skills? Observe, Describe, and Participate
- How do I practice core mindfulness skills? Non-Judgmentally, One-Mindfully, and Effectively

Observe: When observing something, focus on both the internal and external, examining what is going on in the world around you and what is going on in both your body and mind. Practice skills by watching, paying attention to, checking out and noticing. Focus both on individual skills and multiple skills at a time.

Describe: Encourage as many details as possible, both internal and external. Sensory based and descriptive terms for both feelings and thoughts.

Participate: This is a focus on acceptance of that which you are noting, or noticing, paying attention to what you are doing/feeling/thinking without trying to control or change it.

Mindfulness was found to be useful for improving symptoms of mental illness because it helps you analyze and accept your positive and negative experiences and find the most effective solutions. The great thing is… when your mental illness symptoms improve, so does your desire to take care of your physical health!

Your short-term goals for stress reduction:

_____

_____

_____

Your long-term goals for stress reduction:

_____

_____

_____

These are some new stress reduction practices you'd like to try

_____

_____

_____

What's one thing you'll start doing to reduce stress in your life?

_____

_____

_____

What about journaling? Ever tried it? It can be as simple as jotting down your thoughts and feelings for the week/month or as awesome as tracking your moods and the things involved with them on the daily. If you're feeling pretty advantageous, try out Mood Journal Plus, which incorporates all aspects of your mental, emotional, and physical health while bringing some creativity into your life.

Consider downloading an app to help you with stress reduction. There are many free apps you can use from the Apple© or Android© stores for meditation, stress reduction, practicing mindfulness, and more.

Ten Ways you can end stress:

1. Prioritize

_____
_____
_____

2. Social support

_____
_____
_____

3. Accept help

_____
_____
_____

4. "Me time"

_____
_____
_____

5. Organization

_____
_____
_____

6. Limits

_____
_____
_____

7. Mindfulness

_____
_____
_____

8. Nutrition

_____
_____
_____

9. Self-efficacy

_____
_____
_____

10. *Using this handbook!*

NOTES ALONG YOUR JOURNEY:

INTEGRATIVE THERAPY

What? You've never even heard of integrative therapy. That's okay, I'll help you out. Integrative therapy combines Western and Eastern medicine. "Okay, now I'm really confused," you're thinking. Western medicine includes your regular doctors and treatments (the "medical" field) and Eastern medicine includes more "natural" methods.

Let's talk a little about Eastern medicine and how it can complement the treatment you're receiving from your behavioral health practitioner. Integrative therapy, especially when combined with medical treatment, further promotes the internal environment over the outer environment. Think about promoting healing intention, personal wholeness, healing relationships and organizations, healthy lifestyles, and resilience. The foundations of integrative therapy include relationship-centered care, healing space, self-care, intention and awareness, collaborative care, lifestyle, and spiritual connection. Still confused? Let's break down the most popular integrative therapies.

Reiki   ☐ TRY IT?

Reiki is a healing energy-type of therapy that takes care of your breathing, circulation, digestion, cognition, and more without lifting a finger. Reiki helps the body and mind heal itself especially when faced with certain amounts of stress. Ongoing stress, such as dealing with a mental illness, sometimes prevents the body from self-regulating. Reiki helps to channel positive energy into the body where trained practitioners typically place their hands on the body where a powerful flow of positive energy fulfills the body and mind and releases stress, while improving the immunity. Reiki energies have healthy frequency and does not involve taking additional pills or adding a regimen to your already full plate.

Crystal Healing   ☐ TRY IT?

Crystal healing is an alternative technique that uses semi-precious stones and crystals such as quartz and amethyst. Using crystals can boost low energy, prevent bad energy, and release blocked energy. There are a variety of methods to use crystals such as placing them around your body, on your body, or just by simply holding them. It has been said that crystals also help by increasing the body's "vibrations" which help align your mind, body, and spirit. Some even wear the crystals.

Aromatherapy
☐ TRY IT?

Aromatic plants have been used since the dawn of history. Now we use essential oils to maintain and promote physical, psychological, and spiritual wellbeing. Essential oils are substances that occur naturally in a variety of plants growing all over the world. They can be used in massage, ointments/creams, compress, steam inhalation, bath, and vaporization. You may have heard of lavender. It is most often used for tension, sleep, anxiety, and agitation and has a cool and soothing characteristic.

Acupuncture
☐ TRY IT?

Acupuncture is a traditional Chinese medicine where needles are inserted into the body. While is it most often used as a source of pain relief, it can be used for a wide range of others such as emotional stress. Acupuncture is performed by trained practitioners using a clean needle technique and single use needles. Similar to acupressure where physical pressure is applied to "pressure points" by the hand or elbow, acupuncture uses clean needles to access acupuncture points that potentially leads to healing within certain areas.

Chakra Clearing
☐ TRY IT?

Your thoughts and habits control the energy flow within and around you. Different energy centers within and around your body are influenced by your habits. While your body has a lot of chakras, there are seven main chakras, which I'll explain below.

The major chakras that affect your life are located deep within the center of your body. The Root Chakra is located at the base of your spine, which affect career, home, physical safety, and needs. The Sacral Chakra is found midway between your navel and the base of your spine. This is affected by cravings for physical pleasure, addictions, and your body. The Solar Plexus Chakra is found right behind the navel. It is affected by power and control. The Heart Chakra is located in the center of the chest and is affected by relationships, love, attachments, and forgiveness. The Throat Chakra is in the Adam's apple area and is affected by speaking your truth, communication, wanting needs to be met. The Third-Eye is located between the two eyes and is affected by the future, the past, and spiritual guidance. The Crown Chakra is found near the inside of the top of the head and is affected by religion and spirituality, guidance, and trust.

With cleansed and balanced chakras, you can easily relax, accept help from others, and feel more motivated. Chakra clearing can be while brushing your teeth, grocery shopping, taking a nap, etc.

Gosh, that's a lot! Do you have to understand ALL of this? No, of course not; however, the fact is that energy psychology and other integrative methods help you both mentally and physically and even spiritually (if that's of interest to you). Healthy Mind + Healthy Body = Healthy YOU

Which of the above methods are you interested in trying?

_____

_____

_____

_____

What is one that you commit to trying to promote your wellness?

_____

_____

_____

_____

What are some goals in relation to learning more about these methods?

_____

_____

_____

_____

Still sound intimidating? Take a little time to research. YouTube(c) is a great tool to find meditative music/sounds to help balance and align your chakras. Brenda, an eminent Reiki Master, once told me that if your Root Chakra is "balanced" you will be more grounded, which helps you ward off the negative energy surrounding life, illness, happiness, and more. Don't let the chakras scare you. You can easily align any and all of them by using simple yoga poses, stretches, or positive affirmations.

Allow me to go more in-depth...

CHAKRAS SYSTEM *next page*

If you feel like this is too overwhelming, or perhaps you cannot locate local resources regarding integrative therapies, just remember that it doesn't have to be extravagant or cost a lot of money. Simple stretching, meditation, music, and relaxation will help.

CHAKRAS

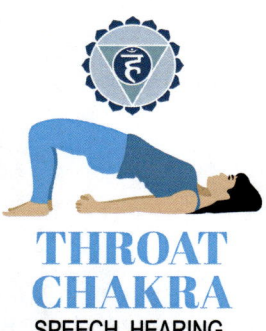

THROAT CHAKRA
SPEECH, HEARING, SELF-EXPRESSION.

Location:
Throat / Base of Neck
Scent: Lavender
Yoga Pose: Bridge Pose
Crystal: Lapis Lazuli

CROWN CHAKRA
DETACHMENT FROM EGO, ENLIGHTENMENT

Location: Top of Head
Scent: Jasmine
Yoga Pose: Lotus Pose
Crystal: Amethyst

THIRD EYE CHAKRA
MIND & BODY COVERAGE, DECISION-MAKING, INTUITION

Location:
Forehead / Between Eyebrows
Scent: Vanilla
Yoga Pose: Easy Pose
Crystal: Sodalite

SYSTEM

SOLAR PLEXUS CHAKRA

POWER, PURPOSE, SELF-ESTEEM

Location:
Midway between Solar Plexus &
Base of Sternum
Scent: Lemon
Yoga Pose:
Half Lord of the Fishes Pose
Crystal: Citrine

HEART CHAKRA

SEAT OF THE SOUL,
EMPATHY, LOVE

Location: Center of Chest
Scent: Eucalyptus
Yoga Pose: Cobra Pose
Crystal: Jade

ROOT CHAKRA

GROUNDED, SECURE,
PROSPEROUS

Location: Base of Spine
Scent: Vetiver
Yoga Pose: Warrior Pose
Crystal: Black Tourmaline

SACRAL CHAKRA

CREATIVITY, EMOTIONAL
STABILITY, FLEXIBILITY

Location: Lower Abdomen
Scent: Tangerine
Yoga Pose:
Wide-Angle Seated Forward Bend
Crystal: Carnellan

Lifestyle Change
CONTRACT

I, _____ , HAVE DECIDED TO WORK
ON A HEALTHIER ME. I ACCEPT THE CHALLENGE AND
UNDERSTAND THAT TAKING CARE OF MYSELF AND
BECOMING HEALTHY ARE MY OWN RESPONSIBILITIES.
I AM AWARE THAT TAKING CARE OF MYSELF IS A
POSITIVE STEP IN MY OWN SELF-CARE AND WELLNESS.

SIGNATURE: DATE:

_____   _____

WITNESS: DATE:

_____   _____

CHALLENGE

Week 1

What I changed:
_____
_____
_____

How I felt:
_____
_____
_____

Week 2

What I changed:
_____
_____
_____

How I felt:
_____
_____
_____

Week 3

What I changed:
_____
_____
_____

How I felt:
_____
_____
_____

Week 4

What I changed:
_____
_____
_____

How I felt:
_____
_____
_____

LETTER TO YOURSELF

Write yourself a letter that explains all the reasons you're deciding to change your lifestyle. What do you think you're going to enjoy? Why do you think you need this? Take a little time to write this note to yourself:

Dear Me,

_____

_____

_____

_____

_____

_____

_____

_____

_____

_____

_____

_____

_____

_____

_____

_____

_____

_____

_____

_____

_____

_____

_____

_____

_____

JOURNAL

Thoughts and feelings as I work on my healthier lifestyle

GRAINS Make half your grains whole	VEGETABLES Vary your veggies	FRUITS Focus on fruits	MILK Get your calcium-rich foods	MEAT & BEANS Go lean with protein
Eat at least 3 oz. of whole-grain cereals, breads, crackers, rice, or pasta every day 1 oz. is about 1 slice of bread, about 1 cup of breakfast cereal, or ½ cup of cooked rice, cereal, or pasta	Eat more dark-green veggies like broccoli, spinach, and other dark leafy greens Eat more orange vegetables like carrots and sweetpotatoes Eat more dry beans and peas like pinto beans, kidney beans, and lentils	Eat a variety of fruit Choose fresh, frozen, canned, or dried fruit Go easy on fruit juices	Go low-fat or fat-free when you choose milk, yogurt, and other milk products If you don't or can't consume milk, choose lactose-free products or other calcium sources such as fortified foods and beverages	Choose low-fat or lean meats and poultry Bake it, broil it, or grill it Vary your protein routine — choose more fish, beans, peas, nuts, and seeds

For a 2,000-calorie diet, you need the amounts below from each food group. To find the amounts that are right for you, go to MyPyramid.gov.

Eat 6 oz. every day	Eat 2½ cups every day	Eat 2 cups every day	Get 3 cups every day; for kids aged 2 to 8, it's 2	Eat 5½ oz. every day

Find your balance between food and physical activity

- Be sure to stay within your daily calorie needs.
- Be physically active for at least 30 minutes most days of the week.
- About 60 minutes a day of physical activity may be needed to prevent weight gain.
- For sustaining weight loss, at least 60 to 90 minutes a day of physical activity may be required.
- Children and teenagers should be physically active for 60 minutes every day, or most days.

Know the limits on fats, sugars, and salt (sodium)

- Make most of your fat sources from fish, nuts, and vegetable oils.
- Limit solid fats like butter, margarine, shortening, and lard, as well as foods that contain these.
- Check the Nutrition Facts label to keep saturated fats, trans fats, and sodium low.
- Choose food and beverages low in added sugars. Added sugars contribute calories with few, if any, nutrients.

RESOURCES

Arvidsdotter, T., Marklund, B., & Taft, C. (2014). Six-month effects of integrative treatment therapeutic acupuncture and conventional treatment in alleviating psychological distress in primary care patients - Follow up from an open, pragmatic randomized controlled trial. BMC Complementary and Alternative Medicine, 14(210), 1-10. doi: 10.1186/1472-6882-14-210

Chadwick, A., Street, C., McAndrew, S., & Deacon, M. (2012). Minding our own bodies: Reviewing the literature regarding the perceptions of service users diagnosed with serious mental illness on barriers to accessing physical health care. International Journal of Mental Health Nursing, 21(3), 211-219. doi: 10.1111/j.1447-0349.2011.00807.x

Cook, B. L., Wayne, G. F., Kafali, N., Liu, Z., & Shu, C. (2014). Trends in smoking among adults with mental illness and association between mental health treatment and smoking cessation. Journal of the American Medical Association, 311(2), 172-182. doi: 10.1001/jama.2013.284985

Evins, A. E., Cather, C., & Laffer, A. (2015). Treatment of tobacco use disorders in smokers with serious mental illness: Toward clinical best practices. Harvard Review of Psychiatry, 23(2), 90-98. doi: 10.1097/HRP.0000000000000063

Ferraresi, M., Clari, R., Moro, I., Banino, E., Boero, E., Crosio, A., Dayne, R., Rosset, L. Scarpa, A., Serra, E., Surace, A., Testore, A., Colombi, N., & Giorgina, B. (2013). Reiki and related therapies in the dialysis ward: An evidence-based and ethical discussion to debate if these complementary and alternative medicines are welcomed or banned. BMC Nephrology, 14(1), 1-7. doi: 10.1186/1471-2369-14-129

Gower, B. A., & Goss, A. M. (2015). A lower-carbohydrate, higher-fat diet reduces abdominal and intermuscular fat and increases insulin sensitivity in adults at risk of type 2 diabetes. Journal of Nutrition, 145(1), 177S-183S. doi: 10.3945/ jn.114.195065

Naslund, J. A., Whiteman, K. L., McHugo, G. J., Aschbrenner, K. A., Marsch, L. A., & Bartels, S. J. (2017). Lifestyle interventions for weight loss among overweight and obese adults with serious mental illness: A systematic review and meta-analysis. General Hospital Psychiatry, 47, 83-102. doi: 10.1016/ j.genhosppsych.2017.04.003

National Institute of Mental Health. (2021). Mental illness. https://www.nimh.nih.gov/health/statistics/mental-illness.shtml

Potes, A., Souza, G., Nikolitch, K., Penheiro, R., Moussa, Y., Jarvis, E., Looper, K., & Rej, S. (2018). Mindfulness in severe and persistent mental illness: A systematic review. International Journal of Psychiatry in Clinical Practice, 22(4), 253-261. doi:10.1080/13651501.2018.1433857

Rakel, D. (2018). Integrative medicine. Philadelphia, PA: Elsevier.

Richardson, C. R., Faulkner, G., McDevitt, J., Skrinar, G. S., Hutchinson, D. S., & Piette, J. D. (2005). Integrating physical activity into mental health services for persons with serious mental illness. Psychiatric Services, 56(3), 324-331. doi: 10.1176/appi.ps.56.3.324

Schmutte, T., Davidson, L., & O'Connell, M. (2018). Improved sleep, diet, and exercise in adults with serious mental illness: Results from a pilot self-management intervention. Psychiatric Quarterly, 89(1), 61-71. doi: 10.1007/s11126-017-9516-9

Tam, J., Warner, K., & Meza, R. (2016). Smoking and the reduced life expectancy of individuals with serious mental illness. American Journal of Preventative Medicine, 51(6), 958-966. doi: 10.1016/j.amepre.2016.06.007

Wazni, L., & Gifford, W. (2017). Addressing physical health needs of individuals with schizophrenia using Orem's theory. Journal of Holistic Nursing, 35(3), 271-279. doi: 10.1177/0898010116658366

Whiteman, K. L., Naslund, J. A., DiNapoli, E. A., Bruce, M. L., & Bartels, S. J. (2016). Systematic review of integrated general medical and psychiatric self-management interventions for adults with serious mental illness. Psychiatric Services, 67(11), 1213-1225. doi: 10.1176/appi.ps.201500521

ABOUT THE AUTHOR

Erica is a Doctor of Psychology who specializes in substance abuse counseling, mental health advocacy, education, and human services. She operates an integrated residential living system for adults with mental illnesses and substance use disorders. Erica has extensive education in the fields of psychology, health care, and business.

Erica also lives with mental illness and metabolic syndrome. With family support, integrative therapy, medication, self-care, and hard work, she is living well and is an advocate for individuals in similar situations. Erica's wife, Brenda, is a Reiki Master who has inspired her to use natural methods as a complementary form of treatment. Erica regularly uses crystals, essential oils, and chakra work to ensure whole health and wellness.